Gems From The East

Graphics by Greg C. Grace

ISBN: 1-84013-472-0

Copyright © Axiom Publishing 2001

This edition produced for Grange Books
Units 1-6 Kingsnorth Ind. Est.
Hoo, nr Rochester
Kent ME3 9ND
United Kingdom
www.Grangebooks.co.uk

Grange Books PLC

Gems
from the
East

H. P. Blavatsky

PREFACE

Few words will be needed by way of preface to these "Gems from the East."

At a time when Western minds are occupied in the study of Oriental Literature, attracted possibly by its richness of expression and marvellous imagery, but no less by the broad yet deep philosophy of life, and the sweet altruistic doctrines contained therein, it is thought seasonable to present the public with a useful and attractive little volume such as this.

The Precepts and Aphorisms, compiled by "H.P.B.," are culled chiefly from Oriental writings considered to embody, in part, teachings which are now attracting so much attention in the West, and for the diffusion of which the Theosophical Society is mainly responsible.

As far as possible we have endeavoured to make the volume attractive, handy, and useful to all.

It contains a Precept or an Axiom for every day in the year; lines of a Theosophical nature, selected from sources not invariably Oriental, preface each month.

It is hoped that our efforts will meet with approval from all lovers of the good and beautiful, and that they may not be without effect in the cause of TRUTH.

W.R.O.

"THERE IS NO RELIGION HIGHER THAN TRUTH"

H. P. BLAVATSKY

"Helena Petrovna Blavatsky...is surely among the most original and perceptive minds of her time...[In her two major books]....lies...the first philosophy of psychic and spiritual evolution to appear in the West...."

Theodore Roszak. The Unfinished Animal 1975

Helena Petrovna Blavatsky was born on August 12, 1831, at Dnepropetrovsk in the Ukraine.

In 1873 she travelled to New York from Paris where, she tried to interest Spiritualists in the philosophy behind phenomena but they resented her refusal to accept their standard explanations. In 1875 she became the principal founder of The Theosophical Society. She devoted the rest of her life to its humanitarian and educational objectives.

JANUARY.

"Uttishat! — Rise! Awake!
Seek the great Teachers, and attend! The road
Is narrow as a knife-edge! Hard to tread!
But whoso once perceiveth Him that Is:—
Without a name, unseen, impalpable,
Bodiless, undiminished, unenlarged,
To senses undeclared, without an end,
Without beginning, timeless, higher than height,
Deeper than depth! Lo! Such one is saved!
Death hath not power upon him!".

—THE SECRET OF DEATH (from: The Katha Upanishad).

1 The first duty taught in Theosophy, is to do one's duty unflinchingly by every duty.

2 The heart which follows the rambling senses leads away his judgment as the wind leads a boat astray upon the waters.

3 He who casts off all desires, living free from attachments, and free from egoism, obtains bliss.

4 To every man that is born, an axe is born in his mouth, by which the fool cuts himself, when speaking bad language.

5 As all earthen vessels made by the potter end in being broken, so is the life of mortals.

6 Wise men are light-bringers.

7 A just life, a religious life, this is the best gem.

8 Having tasted the sweetness of illusion and tranquillity, one becomes free from fear, and free from sin, drinking in the sweetness of Dhamma (law).

9 False friendship is like a parasitic plant, it kills the tree it embraces.

10 Cut out the love of self, like an autumn lotus, with thy hand! Cherish the road of peace.

11 Men who have not observed proper discipline, and have not gained treasure in their youth, perish like old herons in a lake without fish.

12 As the bee collects nectar, and departs without injuring the flower, or its colour or scent, so let a Sage dwell in his village.

13 As rain does not break through a well-thatched house, passion will not break through a well-reflecting mind.

14 He who hath too many friends, hath as many candidates for enemies.

15 That man alone is wise, who keeps the mastery of himself.

16 Seek refuge in thy soul; have there thy Heaven! Scorn them that follow virtue for her gifts!

17 All our dignity consists in thought, therefore let us contrive to think well; for that is the principle of morals.

18 Flattery is a false coin which circulates only because of our vanity.

19 Narrowness of mind causes stubbornness; we do not easily believe what is beyond that which we see.

20 The soul ripens in tears.

21 This is truth the poet sings — That a sorrow's crown of sorrows / Is remembering happier things.

22 Musk is musk because of its own fragrance, and not from being called a perfume by the druggist.

23 Not every one ready for a dispute is as quick in transacting business.

24 It is not every graceful form that contains as graceful a disposition.

25 If every pebble became a priceless ruby, then pebble and ruby would become equal in value.

26 Every man thinks his own wisdom faultless, and every mother her own child beautiful.

27 If wisdom were to vanish suddenly from the universe, no one yet would suspect himself a fool.

28 A narrow stomach may be filled to its satisfaction, but a narrow mind will never be satisfied, not even with all the riches of the world.

29 He who neglects his duty to his conscience, will neglect to pay his debt to his neighbour.

30 Mite added to mite becomes a great heap; the heap in the barn consists of small grains.

31 He who tasteth not thy bread during thy lifetime, will not mention thy name when thou art dead.

FEBRUARY.

"Behold, we know not anything;
I can but trust that good shall fall
At last — far off — at last, to all,
And every winter change to spring.

"So runs my dream: but what am I?
An infant crying in the night:
An infant crying for the light:
And with no language but a cry."

—TENNYSON (In Memoriam)

1 Two things are impossible in this world of Maya: to enjoy more than Karma hath allotted; to die before one's hour hath struck.

2 A student without inclination for work is like a squirrel on its wheel; he makes no progress.

3 A traveller without observation is a bird without wings.

4 A learned man without pupils, is a tree which bears no fruit; a devotee without good works, is a dwelling without a door.

5 When Fate overtakes us, the eye of Wisdom becomes blind.

6 Keep thine eyes open, or Fate will open them for thee.

7 He who kisses the hand he cannot cut off, will have his head cut off by the hand he now kisses in the next rebirth.

8 He who keeps to his business, he who loves his companions, he who does his duty, will never be poor.

9 A thousand regrets will not pay thy debts.

10 Fallen flowers do not return to their stems, nor departed friends to their houses.

11 To feel one's ignorance is to be wise; to feel sure of one's wisdom is to be a fool.

12 One proof is better than ten arguments.

13 Rain in the morn brings the sun after noon. He who weeps today, may laugh tomorrow.

14 The soothsayer for evil never knows his own fate.

15 Like oil, truth often floats on the surface of the lie. Like clear water, truth often underlies the seeming falsehood.

16 Often vinegar got for nothing, is sweeter to the poor man than honey bought.

17 Every tree hath its shadow, every sorrow its joy.

18 The fields are damaged by weeds, mankind by passion. Blessed are the patient, and the passionless.

19 The virtuous man who is happy in this life, is sure to be still happier in his next.

20 What ought to be done is neglected, what ought not to be done is done. The sins of the unruly are ever increasing.

21 Without Karma, no fisherman could catch a fish; outside of Karma, no fish would die on dry land, or in boiling water.

22 Let every man first become himself that which he teaches others to be.

23 He who hath subdued himself, may hope to subdue others. One's own self is the most difficult to master.

24 Hatred is never quenched by hatred; hatred ceases by showing love; this is an old rule.

25 The path of virtue lies in the renunciation of the seven great sins.

26 The best possession of the man of clay is health; the highest virtue of the man of spirit is truthfulness.

27 Man walks on, and Karma follows him along with his shadow.

28 Daily practical wisdom consists of four things: — To know the root of Truth, the branches of Truth, the limit of Truth, and the opposite of Truth.

MARCH.

"Say not 'I am,' 'I was,' or 'I shall be,'
Think not ye pass from house to house of flesh
Like travellers who remember and forget,
Ill-lodged or well-lodged. Fresh
Issues upon the universe that sum
Which is the lattermost of lives. It makes
Its habitation as the worm spins silk
And dwells therein."

—LIGHT OF ASIA, Bk. 8.

1 Four things increase by use: — Health, wealth, perseverance, and credulity.

2 To enjoy the day of plenty, you must be patient in the day of want.

3 Expel avarice from your heart, so shall you loosen the chains from off your neck.

4 Let a man overcome anger by love, evil by good, greediness by liberality, lie by truth.

5 Do not speak harshly to anybody; those who are so spoken to will answer thee in the same way.

6 This life is in the world of work and retributive justice; the life that follows is in the world of great reward.

7 Excuse is better than disputation; delay is better than rashness; unwillingness of strife is better than eagerness in seeking it.

8 Cut down the whole forest of lust, not the tree. When thou hast cut down every tree and every shrub, then thou wilt be free.

9 The avaricious go not to the world of the gods (Devas), for the fool commands no charity.

10 He who holds back rising anger like a rolling chariot, is called a real driver; other people are but holders of the reins.

11 The fool who is angered, and who thinks to triumph by using abusive language, is always vanquished by him whose words are patient.

12 The best of medicines is death; the worst of diseases is vain anticipation.

13 An easy temper is a good counsellor, and a pleasant tongue is an excellent leader.

14 A good word in time is better than a sweet pie after meals.

15 Foolish pride is an incurable malady; a bad wife is a chronic disease; and a wrathful disposition is a life-long burden.

16 Truth is brighter than the sun; Truth is the sunny day of Reason, and falsehood the mind's dark night.

17 All has an end, and will away. Truth alone is immortal, and lives for ever.

18 The light of all flesh is the sun; the light of the soul — truth everlasting.

19 The road to sin is a wide highway; the way out of it, a steep and rugged hill.

20 The fault of others is easily perceived, but that of oneself is difficult to perceive.

21 Good people shine from afar like the snowy mountains; bad people are not seen, like arrows shot at night.

22 Where two women meet, there a market springs; where three congregate, a bazaar is opened; and where seven talk, there begins a fair.

23 Extensive knowledge and science, well-regulated discipline and well-spoken speech, this is the greatest blessing.

24 The subtle self is to be known by thought alone; for every thought of men is interwoven with the senses, and when thought is purified, then the self arises.

25 Lead me from the unreal to the real! Lead me from darkness to light! Lead me from death to immortality!

26 The Sage who knows Brahman moves on; on the small, old path that stretches far away, rests in the heavenly place, and thence moves higher on.

27 Neither by the eyes, nor by spirit, nor by the sensuous organs, nor by austerity, nor by sacrifices, can we see Brahma. Only the pure, by the light of wisdom and meditation, can see the pure Deity.

28 By perfection in study and meditation the Supreme Spirit becomes manifest; study is one eye to behold it, and meditation is the other.

29 Alas! We reap what seed we sow; the hands that smite us are our own.

30 Thoughts alone cause the round of rebirths in this world; let a man strive to purify his thoughts, what a man thinks, that he is: this is the old secret.

31 "My sons are mine; this wealth is mine": with such thoughts is a fool tormented. He himself does not belong to himself, much less sons and wealth.

APRIL.

"The untouched soul,

Greater than all the worlds (because the worlds

By it subsist); smaller than subtleties

Of things minutest; last of ultimates;

Sits in the hollow heart of all that lives!

Whoso hath laid aside desire and fear,

His senses mastered, and his spirit still,

Sees in the quiet light of verity

Eternal, safe, majestical — HIS SOUL!"

—THE SECRET OF DEATH (fr. The Katha Upanishad).

1 He who leaves the society of fools, cleaves unto the wise.

2 The self is hidden in all beings, and does not shine forth; but it is seen by subtle seers, through their sharp and subtle intellect.

3 Patience leads to power; but eagerness in greed leads to loss.

4 Three things make a poor man rich: courtesy, consideration for others, and the avoidance of suspicion.

5 When trust is gone, misfortune comes in; when confidence is dead, revenge is born; and when treachery appears, all blessings fly away.

6 The world exists by cause; all things exist by cause; and beings are bound by cause, even as the rolling cart-wheel by the pin of an axle-tree.

7 The living soul is not woman, nor man, nor neuter; whatever body it takes, with that it is joined only.

8 He ho wishes to reach Buddhahood, and aspires to the knowledge of the Self-born, must honour those who keep this doctrine.

9 As the spider moving upward by his thread gains free space, thus also he who undertakes moving upward by the known word OM, gains independence.

10 The wheel of sacrifice has Love for its nave, Action for its tire, and Brotherhood for its spokes.

11 Man consists of desires. And as is his desire, so is his will; and as is his will, so is his deed; and whatever deed he does, that he will reap.

12 A stone becomes a plant; a plant a beast; the beast a man; a man a Spirit; and the Spirit — GOD.

13 There exists no spot on the earth, or in the sky, or in the sea, neither is there any in the mountain-clefts, where an evil deed does not bring trouble to the doer.

14 Whoever, not being a sanctified person, pretends to be a Saint, he is indeed the lowest of all men, the thief in all worlds, including that of Brahma.

15 If a man consorting with me (Buddha) does not conform his life to my commandments, what benefit will ten thousand precepts be to him?

16 He who smites will be smitten; he who shows rancour will find rancour; so, from reviling cometh reviling, and to him who is angered comes anger.

17 "He abused me, he reviled me, he beat me, he subdued me"; he who keeps this in mind, and who feels resentment, will find no peace.

18 Like a beautiful flower, full of colour, but without scent, are the fine but fruitless words of him who does not act accordingly.

19 When your mind shall have crossed beyond the taint of delusion, then will you become indifferent to all that you have heard or will hear.

20 The wise guard the home of nature's order; they assume excellent forms in secret.

21 If thou losest all, and gettest wisdom by it, thy loss is thy gain.

22 Empty thy mind of evil, but fill it with good.

23 Great works need no great strength, but perseverance.

24 Sleep is but birth into the land of Memory; birth but a sleep in the oblivion of the Past.

25 To forgive without forgetting, is again to reproach the wrong-doer every time the act comes back to us.

26 Every man contains within himself the potentiality of immortality, equilibrated by the power of choice.

27 He who lives in one colour of the rainbow is blind to the rest. Live in the light diffused through the entire arc, and you will know it all.

28 Every time the believer pronounces the word OM, he renews the allegiance to the divine potentiality enshrined within the Soul.

29 People talk of the Devil. Every man has seen him; he is in every sinful heart.

30 The Higher Self knows that highest home of Brahman, which contains all and shines so bright. The wise who without desiring happiness worship that SELF, are not born again.

MAY.

I'm weary of conjectures, — this must end 'em.

Thus am I doubly armed: my death and life,

My bane and antidote, are both before me:

This in a moment brings me to an end;

But this informs me I shall never die.

The Soul, secured in her existence, smiles

At the drawn dagger, and defies its point.

The stars shall fade away, the sun himself

Grow dim with age, and nature sink in years;

But thou shalt flourish in immortal youth,

Unhurt amidst the war of elements,

The wrecks of matter, and the crush of worlds.

—ADDISON.

1 The eternal Spirit is everywhere. It stands encompassing the whole world.

2 He who feeds the hungry before he has assuaged his own hunger, prepares for himself eternal food. He who renounces that food for the sake of a weaker brother is — a god.

3 The altar on which the sacrifice is offered is Man; the fuel is speech itself, the smoke the breath, the light the tongue, the coals the eye, the sparks the ear.

4 One moment in eternity is as important as another moment, for eternity changeth not, neither is one part better than another part.

5 Better it would be that a man should eat a lump of flaming iron than that one should break his vows.

6 Even a good man sees evil days, as long as his good deeds have not ripened; but when they have ripened, then does the good man see happy days.

7 By oneself the evil is done, by oneself one suffers; by oneself the evil is left undone, by oneself one is purified.

8 Purity and impurity belong to oneself; no one can purify another.

9 Self is the lord of Self: who else could be the lord! With self well subdued, a man finds a master such as few can find.

10 If one man conquer in battle a thousand times a thousand men, and if another conquer himself, he is the greater of the two conquerors.

11 Who is the great man? He who is strongest in patience. He who patiently endures injury, and maintains a blameless life — he is a man indeed!

12 If thou hast done evil deeds, or if thou wouldst do them, thou mayest arise and run where'er thou wilt, but thou canst not free thyself of thy suffering.

13 There is a road that leads to Wealth; there is another road that leads to Nirvana.

14 An evil deed does not turn on a sudden like curdling milk; it is like fire smouldering in the ashes, which burns the fool.

15 An evil deed kills not instantly, as does a sword, but it follows the evil-doer into his next and still next rebirth.

16 The calumniator is like one who flings dirt at another when the wind is contrary, the dirt does but return on him who threw it.

17 The virtuous man cannot be hurt, the misery that his enemy would inflict comes back on himself.

18 Nature is upheld by antagonism. Passions, resistance, danger, are educators. We acquire the strength we have overcome.

19 If a man understands the self saying "I am He," what could he wish or desire that he should pine after the body?

20 That word which all the Vedas record, which all penances proclaim, which men desire when they live as religious disciples, that word I tell thee briefly, it is OM.

21 As a person having seen one in a dream, recognises him afterwards; so does one who has achieved proper concentration of mind perceive the SELF.

22 It is better to do one's own duty, even though imperfectly, than to perform another's duty well.

23 The wise who knows the Self as bodiless within the bodies, as unchanging among changing things, as great and omnipresent, does never grieve.

24 The path of virtue lies in the renunciation of arrogance and pride.

25 He who wrongs another unjustly will regret it, though men may applaud him; but he who is wronged is safe from regret, though the world may blame him.

26 There is more courage in facing the world with undisguised truth, than in descending into a wild beast's den.

27 True clemency is in foregoing revenge, when it is in one's power; true patience is in bearing up against disappointments.

28 The happy man must prepare ere the evil day comes; and when it does, let the thought that every good and great man has been made to suffer at some time console him.

29 Wealth in the hands of one who thinks not of helping mankind with it, is sure to turn one day into dry leaves.

30 Like as the night follows the day, so misfortune is the shadow of joy; Karma bestowing her lots with both hands.

31 The eagle catcheth not flies; but even the eagle is disturbed by them.

JUNE.

"There is true Knowledge. Learn thou it is this:

To see one Changeless Life in all that lives,
And in the Separate, One Inseparable.
There is imperfect Knowledge: that which sees
The separate existences apart,
And, being separated, holds them real.
There is false Knowledge: that which blindly clings
To one as if 'twere all, seeking no cause,
Deprived of light, narrow, and dull, and dark."

—SONG CELESTIAL, Bk. 18 (fr. The Bhagavad-Gita)

1 Judge the tree by its fruits, man by his deeds.

2 Theosophy is not the acquirement of powers, whether psychic or intellectual, though both are its servants.

3 Neither is Theosophy the pursuit of happiness, as men understand the word; for the first step is sacrifice, the second, renunciation.

4 Life is built up by the sacrifice of the individual to the whole. Each cell in the living body must sacrifice itself to the perfection of the whole; when it is otherwise, disease and death enforce the lesson.

5 Theosophy is the science of life, the art of living.

6 Harmony is the law of life, discord its shadow; whence springs suffering, the teacher, the awakener of consciousness.

7 Through joy and sorrow, pain and pleasure, the soul comes to a knowledge of itself.

8 The eyes of wisdom are like the ocean depths; there is neither joy nor sorrow in them. Therefore the soul of the disciple must become stronger than joy, and greater than sorrow.

9 We hate but those whom we envy or fear.

10 Self-knowledge is unattainable by what men usually call "self-analysis." It is not reached by reasoning or any brain-powers.

11 Real self-knowledge is the awakening to consciousness of the divine nature of man.

12 Will is the offspring of the Divine, the God in man; Desire, the motive power of the animal life.

13 Will is the exclusive possession of man. It divides him from the brute, in whom instinctive desire only is active.

14 To obtain the knowledge of self, is a greater achievement than to command the elements or to know the future.

15 The great watchword of the True is this — in last analysis all things are divine.

16 Fear is the slave of Pain, and Rebellion her captive.

17 Endurance is the free companion of Sorrow, and Patience her master.

18 The husband of Pain is Rapture, but the souls are few in whom that marriage is consummated.

19 Spirituality is not what we understand by the words "virtue" and "goodness." It is the power of perceiving formless, spiritual essences.

20 The discovery and right use of the true essence of Being — this is the whole secret of life.

21 When desire is for the purely abstract — when it has lost all trace or tinge of "self" — then it has become pure.

22 Adepts are rare as the blossom of the Udumbara tree.

23 The one eternal, immutable law of life alone can judge and condemn man absolutely.

24 Will and Desire are both absolute creators, forming the man himself and his surroundings.

25 Will creates intelligently; Desire blindly and unconsciously.

26 Man makes himself in the image of his desires, unless he creates himself in the likeness of the Divine, through his will, the child of the light.

27 Theosophy is the vehicle of the spirit that giveth life; consequently, nothing dogmatic can be Theosophical.

28 Some pluck the fruits of the tree of knowledge to crown themselves therewith, instead of plucking them to eat.

29 It is not necessary for truth to put on boxing-gloves.

30 You cannot build a temple of truth by hammering dead stones. Its foundations must precipitate themselves like crystals from the solution of life.

JULY.

"The mind, enlightened, casts its grief away!" —

"It is not to be known by knowledge! man
Wotteth it not by wisdom! learning vast
Halts short of it! Only by soul itself
Is soul perceived — when the soul wills it so!
There shines no light save its own light to show
Itself unto itself!"

—THE SECRET OF DEATH (from The Katha Upanishad).

1 One cannot fill a vacuum from within itself.

2 When a certain point is reached, pain becomes its own anodyne.

3 Many a man will follow a mis-leader. Few will recognise truth at a glance.

4 Esteem that to be eminently good, which, when communicated to another, will be increased to yourself.

5 Be persuaded that those things are not your riches which you do not possess in the penetralia of the reasoning power.

6 As many passions of the soul, so many fierce and savage despots.

7 No one is free who has not obtained the empire of himself.

8 It is the business of a musician to harmonise every instrument, but of a well-educated man to adapt himself harmoniously to every fortune.

9 It is excellent to impede an unjust man; but if this be not possible, it is excellent not to act in conjunction with him.

10 Sin should be abstained from, not through fear, but for the sake of the becoming.

11 Vehement desires about any one thing render the soul blind with respect to other things.

12 Many men who have not learnt to argue rationally, still live according to reason.

13 The equal is beautiful in everything, but excess and defect do not appear so.

14 It is the property of a divine intellect to be always intently thinking about the beautiful.

15 As two pieces of wood may come together in the ocean, and having met, may separate again; like this is the meeting of mortals.

16 Youth is like a mountain-torrent; wealth is like the dust on one's feet; manhood is fugitive as a water-drop; life is like foam.

17 Who fulfills not duty with steadfast mind, duty which opens the portals of bliss, surprised by old age and remorse, he is burned by the fire of grief.

18 Even in a forest hermitage, sin prevails over the unholy; the restraint of the senses in one's own house, this is asceticism.

19 Who performs a right action, free from impurity, the house of that man is a forest hermitage.

20 As the streams of a river flow on, and return not, so pass away the days and nights, taking away the lives of men.

21 Unenduring are youth, beauty, life, wealth, lordship, the society of the beloved; let not the wise be deluded by these.

22 In this world, fugitive as tempest-driven waves, death for another is a rich prize earned by virtue in a former birth.

23 The shadows of a cloud, the favour of the base, new corn, a flower, these last only a little time; so it is with youth and riches.

24 Let the wise think on wisdom as unfading and immortal; let him fulfill his duty as though Death grasped him by the hair.

25 If evil be said of thee, and if it be true, correct thyself; if it be a lie, laugh at it.

26 Pagodas are measured by their shadows, and great men by their enviers.

27 The sage does not say what he does; but he does nothing that cannot be said.

28 The man who finds pleasure in vice, and pain in virtue, is still a novice in both.

29 The wise man does good as naturally as he breathes.

30 He is a man who does not turn away from what he has said.

31 The heart of the fool is in his tongue; the tongue of the wise is in his heart.

AUGUST.

"Death has no power th' immortal soul to slay,
That, when its present body turns to clay
Seeks a fresh home, and with unlessened might
Inspires another frame with life and light.
So I myself (well I the past recall),
When the fierce Greeks begirt Troy's holy wall,
Was brave Euphorbus: and in conflict drear
Poured forth my blood beneath Atrides' spear.
The shield this arm did bear I lately saw
In Juno's shrine, a trophy of that war."

—DRYDEN'S OVID

1 The man who neglects the truth he finds in his soul, in order to follow its dead-letter, is a time-server.

2 He who does not recognise the bread and salt is worse than a wild wolf.

3 Man who has not hesitated to project his image in space and call it the Creator, sculpted not to endow God with his own vices.

4 He who has been once deceived, dreads evil, and suspects it even in truth.

5 Krishna, the golden-haired god, replied not to the reviling of the King of Chedi. To the roar of the tempest, and not to the jackal's howl, the elephant trumpets a reply.

6 Not the tender pliant grass is uprooted by the storm, but the lofty trees. The mighty war only with the mighty.

7 The sandal tree has snakes; the lotus tank, alligators; in happiness there is envy. There are no unmixed pleasures.

8 No creature, no thing is free from evil. The sandal tree has its roots sapped by snakes, its blossoms attacked by bees, its branches broken by monkeys, its top eaten by bears. No part of it is secure from pain.

9 Grieve not about thy sustenance; nature will supply it. When a creature is born, the mother's breast supplies milk.

10 Who gave the swan his whiteness, the parrot his wings of golden green, the peacock his iris-hues? Will not that which provided for them provide for thee?

11 All good fortune belongs to him of contented mind. Is not the whole earth leather-covered for him who wears shoes?

12 This world is a venomous tree, bearing two honey-sweet fruits: the divine essence of poetry and the friendship of the noble.

13 By the fall of water-drops the pitcher is gradually filled; this is the cause of wisdom, of virtue, and of wealth.

14 Let one who would live in the memory of his fellow men, make every day fruitful by generosity, study, and noble arts.

15 No plunge in clear cool water delights so much the heat-oppressed, no pearl necklace the maiden, as the words of the good delight the good.

16 Good men vary. Some are like coconuts, full of sweet milk; others, like the jujube, externally pleasing.

17 Like an earthen vessel, easy to break, hard to reunite, are the wicked; the good are like vessels of gold, hard to break and quickly united.

18 Be not a friend to the wicked — charcoal when hot, burns; when cold, it blackens the fingers.

19 Shun him who secretly slanders, and praises openly; he is like a cup of poison, with cream on the surface.

20 A chariot cannot go on one wheel alone; so destiny fails unless men's acts co-operate.

21 The noble delight in the noble; the base do not; the bee goes to the lotus from the wood; not so the frog, though living in the same lake.

22 Like moonbeams trembling on water, truly such is the life of mortals. Knowing this, let duty be performed.

23 Bathe in the river of the soul, O man, for not with water is the soul washed clean.

24 The pure soul is a river whose holy source is self-control, whose water is truth, whose bank is righteousness, whose waves are compassion.

25 Of a gift to be received or given, of an act to be done, time drinks up the flavour, unless it be quickly performed.

26 When the weak-minded is deprived of wealth, his actions are destroyed, like rivulets dried up in hot seasons.

27 He who wants a faultless friend, must remain friendless.

28 Eat and drink with your friends, but do not trade with them.

29 Without trouble one gets no honey. Without grief and sorrow no one passes his life.

30 Vinegar does not catch a fly, but honey. A sweet tongue draweth the snake forth from the earth.

31 What good is advice to a fool?

SEPTEMBER.

"Shall there not be as good a then as now?
Haply much better. . . Therefore fear I not;
And therefore, Holy Sir! my life is glad,
Nowise forgetting yet those other lives
Painful and poor, wicked and miserable,
Whereon the Gods grant pity! But for me,
What good I see, humbly I seek to do,
And live obedient to the law, in trust
That what will come, and must come, shall come well."

—LIGHT OF ASIA, Bk. 6.

1 To him who has subdued self by SELF, his self is a friend; but to him who has not subdued senses by mind, that self is an enemy.

2 The eye is a window which looks into the heart. The brain is a door through which heart escapes.

3 Devotion and clear vision are not his who eats too much, nor his who eats not at all; not his who sleeps too much, nor his who is too awake.

4 At the end of a life of study, the man possessed of knowledge approaches Deity; and at the end of many lives, the wise man becomes one with the ALL.

5 Grief and wrath, avarice and desire, delusion and laziness, vindictiveness and vanity, envy and hatred, censoriousness and slander — are the twelve sins destructive of man's bliss.

6 The wolf changes his coat, and the serpent his skin, but not their nature.

7 The young of the raven appears to it a nightingale.

8 The dog howls at the moon, but the moon heeds it not; be like the moon.

9 Let your soul work in harmony with the universal intelligence, as your breath does with the air.

10 Let no bitterness find entrance into the heart of a mother.

11 Pervert not the heart of a man who is pure, for he will turn thine own first enemy.

12 Do not make a wicked man thy companion, or act on the advice of a fool.

Gems From The East

13 Save not thy life at the expense of another's, as he will take two of thy lives in future births.

14 Mock not the deformed; assume not a proud demeanor with thy inferiors; hurt not the feelings of the poor; be kind to those weaker than thyself, and charitable to all beings.

15 Sacrifice not thy weaker child to the stronger, but protect him.

16 Amuse not thyself at the expense of those who depend on thee. Mock not a venerable man, for he is thy superior. .

17 Death is a black camel that kneels at everybody's door. Death is a friend and a deliverer.

18 A little hill in a low place thinks itself a great mountain.

19 Men are gnomes condemned to forced toils in the kingdom of darkness (or ignorance).

20 We are the true troglodytes, cave-dwellers, though we call our cavern the world.

21 Living for ages in the night-realm, we dream that our darkness is full day.

22 All life is but a perpetual promise; an engagement renewed, but never fulfilled.

23 Man is a king, dethroned, and cast out from his kingdom; in chains and in a dungeon.

24 The heart of a beggar will not be content with half the universe; he is not born to a part, but to the whole.

25 Our life is the ante-room of the palace where our true treasure lies — immortality.

26 Useless to seek to seize the ocean-echo, by clasping the shell in which it lies hid; as useless to try to seize this essence, by grasping the form in which for a moment it shone.

27 When the leaden clouds clash together, the fair glimpse of heaven is shut out.

28 When the silence falls upon us, we can hear the voices of the gods, pointing out in the quiet light of divine law the true path for us to follow.

29 All the air resounds with the presence of spirit and spiritual laws.

30 The spirit it is, that, under the myriad illusions of life, works steadily towards its goal; silently, imperceptibly, irresistibly, moving on to divinity.

OCTOBER.

The consciousness of good, which neither gold,
Nor sordid fame, nor hope of heavenly bliss,
Can purchase; but a life of resolute good,
Unalterable will, quenchless desire
Of universal happiness; the heart
That beats with it in unison; the brain
Whose ever-wakeful wisdom toils to change
Reason's rich stores for its eternal weal.
This "commerce" of sincerest virtue needs
No mediative signs of selfishness,
No jealous intercourse of wretched gain,
No balancings of prudence, cold and long: —
In just and equal measure all is weighed;
One scale contains the sum of human weal,
And one, THE GOOD MAN'S HEART!

—SHELLEY.

1 The glamour of Time conceals from the weak souls of men the dark abysses around them, the terrible and mighty laws which incessantly direct their lives.

2 There is no death without sin, and no affliction without transgression.

3 Man's actions are divided, as regards their object, into four classes; they are either purposeless, unimportant, or vain, or good.

4 The sun causes day and night, divine and human. Night is for the sleep of beings, day for the performance of their duty.

5 If we were convinced that we could never make our crooked ways straight, we should forever continue in our errors.

6 Where there are not virtue and discrimination, learning is not to be sown there, no more than good seed in barren soil.

7 A teacher is more venerable than ten sub-teachers; a father, than one hundred teachers; a mother, than a thousand fathers.

8 Let not a man, even though pained, be sour-tempered, nor devise a deed of mischief to another.

9 One is not aged because his head is grey: whoever, although a youth, has wisdom, him the gods consider an elder.

10 A wise man should ever shrink from honour as from poison, and should always be desirous of disrespect as if of ambrosia.

11 Though despised, one sleeps with comfort, with comfort awakes, with comfort lives in this world; but the scorner perisheth.

12 Trust not in business one ever caught asleep by the sun rising or setting, for thereby he incurs great sin.

13 Those who prefer to swim in the waters of their ignorance, and to go down very low, need not exert the body or heart; they need only cease to move, and they will surely sink.

14 As a man digging comes to water, so a zealous student attains unto knowledge.

15 A good man may receive pure knowledge even from an inferior; the highest virtue from the lowest.

16 Ambrosia may be extracted even from poison; elegant speech even from a fool; virtue even from an enemy; and gold from dross.

17 Whoever offers not food to the poor, raiment to the naked, and consolation to the afflicted, is reborn poor, naked, and suffering.

18 As a sower gets not his harvest if he sow seed in salt soil, so the giver gets no fruit by bestowing on the unworthy.

19 There are three things of which one never tires: health, life and wealth.

20 A misfortune that cometh from on high cannot be averted; caution is useless against the decrees of Fate.

21 The worst of maladies is envy; the best of medicines is health.

22 Three things can never be got with three things: wealth, with wishing for it; youth, with cosmetics; health, with medicine.

23 Trifling ruins earnestness, lying is the enemy of truth, and oppression perverts justice.

24 Caution can never incur disgrace; imbecility can never bring honour with it.

25 Whomsoever riches do not exalt, poverty will not abase, nor calamity cast him down.

26 Night and day are the steeds of man; they hurry him on, not he them.

27 Whoso heeds not a plaint, confesses his own meanness; and whoso makes a merit of his charity, incurs reproach.

28 There are four things of which a little goes on a long way: pain, poverty, error, and enmity.

29 He who knows not his own worth, will never appreciate the worth of others.

30 Whosoever is ashamed of his father and mother, is excluded from the ranks of the wise.

31 He who is not lowly in his own sight, will never be exalted in the sight of others.

NOVEMBER.

"As large as is the unbounded Universe,

So large that little, hidden Spirit is!

The Heavens and Earths are in it! Fire and air,

And sun and moon and stars; darkness and light,

It comprehends! Whatever maketh Man,

The present of him, and the past of him,

And what shall be of him; — all thoughts and things

Lie folded in the eternal vast of It!"

—THE SECRET OF DEATH (fr. The Katha Upanishad).

1 In every blessing think of its end, in every misfortune think of its removal.

2 If justice predominates not over injustice in a man, he will speedily fall into ruin.

3 Vain hopes cut man off from every good; but the renunciation of avarice prevents every ill.

4 Patience leads to power, but lust leads to loss.

5 By wisdom is the gift of knowledge displayed; by knowledge are high things obtained.

6 In calamity are men's virtues proved, and by long absence is their friendship tested.

7 That man who accurately understands the movement and the cause of the revolutions of the wheel of life is never deluded.

8 Days end with sunset, nights with the rising of the sun; the end of pleasure is ever grief, the end of grief ever pleasure.

9 All action ends in destruction; death is certain for whatever is born; everything in this world is transient.

10 In information is shown the wit of man, and in travel is his temper tried.

11 In poverty is benevolence assayed, and in the moment of anger is a man's truthfulness displayed.

12 By truth alone is man' mind purified, and by right discipline it doth become inspired.

13 By shaking hands with deceit, one is tossed on the billows of toil.

14 Fear of judgment will deter from wrong, but trifling with it leads to destruction.

15 An act may seem right, but it is by its results that its purpose is shown.

16 Intelligence is shown by good judgment.

17 Learning clears the mind, and ignorance cobwebs it.

18 Whoso takes good advice is secure from falling; but whoso rejects it, falleth into the pit of his own conceit.

19 By a trusty friend is man supported in life, and by reward are friendships increased.

20 Whoso cannot forgive wrong done to him shall learn to know how his good deeds are undone by himself.

21 He who bestows bounty on mankind, makes of mankind his debtor in a future birth.

22 The envious man is never satisfied, nor can he ever hope to become great.

23 The more a man clothes himself in modesty, the better does he conceal his faults.

24 The best policy for a man is not to boast of his virtues.

25 The kindest policy for a strong man is not to flourish his power in the sight of a weaker man.

26 The contentious man induces antagonism; people cannot often repress anger when contending with fools.

27 Intelligence is not shown by witty words, but by wise actions.

28 Of the eloquence of the pleasant speaker all men are enamored.

29 Craft has the best of men; boldness conquers cities; the first is despised, the last admired.

30 The brave man of whose prowess all men stand in need, will never be distressed by adversaries.

DECEMBER.

"Ring out the old, ring in the new,

Ring, happy bells, across the snow:

The year is going, let him go;

Ring out the false, ring in the true.

"Ring out the grief that saps the mind,

For those that here we see no more;

Ring out the feud of rich and poor,

Ring in redress to all mankind."

—TENNYSON (In Memoriam)

1 The most precious gift received by man on earth is desire for wisdom.

2 In health and wealth man is never in want of friends. True friends, however, are those who remain when they are needed.

3 Of all the animals on earth, man alone has the faculty of causing moral trouble.

4 Man contains three kinds of evil: the evil caused by his (lower) nature; the evil done by man to man; and the evil caused by man to himself.

5 A great man is he who is proof against flattery, vanity, injustice, and the love of pomp and power.

6 The wise man is he who can either take or leave those so-called necessities of life with which other people are intemperate.

7 To hold on with fortitude in one condition, and sobriety in the other, is a proof of a great soul and an impregnable virtue.

8 Let every action be done with perfect gravity, humanity, freedom, and justice, and perform it as though that action were your last.

9 A man can rarely be unhappy by being ignorant of another's thoughts; but he that does not attend to the motions of his own is certainly unhappy.

10 Do not let accidents disturb, or outward objects engross your thoughts; but keep your mind quiet and disengaged, to be ready to learn something good.

11 Manage all your actions, words, and thoughts accordingly, since you can at any moment quit life.

12 What matters dying? If the gods are in being, you can suffer nothing, for they will do you no harm.

13 And if the gods are not, or take no care of mortals — why, then, a world without gods is not worth a man's while to live in.

14 The being of the gods, and their concern in human affairs, is beyond dispute.

15 Remember that life is wearing off, and a smaller part of it is left daily.

16 Depend not upon external supports, nor beg your tranquillity of another. In a word, never throw away your legs to stand upon crutches.

17 If you examine a man that has been well-disciplined and purified by philosophy, you will find nothing that is unsound, false, or foul in him.

18 Life moves in a very narrow compass; yes, and men live in a small corner of the world too.

19 Poor transitory mortals know little even of themselves, much less of those who died long before their time.

20 Death and generation are both mysteries of nature, and resemble each other; the first does but dissolve those elements the latter had combined.

21 Do not suppose you are hurt, and your complaint ceases. Cease your complaint, and you are not hurt.

22 That which does not make man worse, does not make his life worse; as a result, he hath no harm either within or without.

23 At present your nature is distinct; but ere long you will vanish into the whole: you will be returned into that universal reason which gave you your being

24 Do but return to the principles of wisdom, and those who take you now for a monkey or a wild beast will make a god of you.

25 Do not act as if you had ten thousand years to throw away. Death stands at your elbow. Be good for something, while you live, and it is in your power.

26 He that is so anxious about being talked of when he is dead, does not consider that all who knew him will quickly be gone.

27 If you depend too servilely upon the good word of other people, you will be unworthy of your own nature.

28 Whatever is good has that quality from itself; it is finished by its own nature, and commendation is no part of it.

29 Do not run riot; keep your intentions honest, and your convictions sure.

30 He that does a memorable action, and those who report it, are all but short-lived things.

31 Put yourself frankly into the hands of Fate, and let her spin you out what fortune she pleases.

"Scollop style shell or classical Indian design"

The "peacock" is traditionally associated with Lord Krishna
and symbolises, containment of the senses.

The "lotus" is the traditional symbol for purity and the
awakening of inner wisdom.

"Aum" 'the symbol of unity and oneness,
the first primordial sound'.

"A scroll of Classical Indian design".